Join our community!
@ @deardaughters_love_mom
@deardaughters_

Shavon St. Germain
info@deardaughterslovemom.com
www.deardaughterslovemom.com

Dedication

This journal is dedicated to

_____

from

_____

because

_____

_____

_____

Content

NO ONE IS YOU,
AND THAT IS YOUR
POWER.

— DAVE GROHL

Love Yourself

List 10 things you love about yourself.

1. _____
2. _____
3. _____
4. _____
5. _____
6. _____
7. _____
8. _____
9. _____
10. _____

Pick the top 3 words you think others would use to describe you.

1. _____
2. _____
3. _____

Use the scale below to show how much you care about what others think about you.

←« 1	2	3	4	5	6	7	8	9	10 »→
THE LEAST									THE MOST

Explain your answer.

_____

_____

_____

_____

_____

_____

_____

_____

_____

List 3 of your worst characteristics and think about how you can spin them into a positive.

1. _____ »→ _____

    _____

2. _____ »→ _____

    _____

3. _____ »→ _____

    _____

What is something you have always wanted to do but didn't? Why?

THE MEANING OF LIFE IS
TO FIND YOUR GIFT.

THE PURPOSE OF LIFE IS
TO GIVE IT AWAY.

— PABLO PICASSO

Purpose

What brings you joy?

What gifts do you bring?

How do you want to make others feel?

If money wasn't an issue, what would you do with your time?

What problem do you want to solve?

What inspires you?

What would you regret not fully doing, being or having in your life?

What do I want my legacy to be?

THERE IS NO WAY TO BE A
PERFECT MOTHER
AND A MILLION WAYS TO BE
A GOOD ONE

— JILL CHURCHILL

A Mother's Love

How do you feel about being a mother?

How would you describe your mothering style?

What do you love most about being a mother?

What do you love least about being a mother?

What would change about your mothering style?

How do you think your children would describe you as a mother? Not sure? Ask them!

How are you like your mother?

How are you unlike your mother?

How do you feel about your children?

What do you want your children to remember most about you?

FRIENDS COME IN
AND OUT OF YOUR LIFE.

ONLY THE REAL
ONES STAY.

What About Your Friends?

What is your definition of a "friend?"

Do you make friends easily? Why or why not?

_____

_____

_____

_____

_____

_____

_____

_____

_____

_____

_____

_____

_____

_____

List the top 5 qualities you look for in a friend.

1. _____

2. _____

3. _____

4. _____

5. _____

How do you determine who is a "real" friend?

How do you determine how much to share with a friend?

What are your friendship deal breakers?

BECAUSE I HAVE A
SISTER,
I'LL ALWAYS HAVE
A FRIEND.

I Am My Sister's Keeper

What is the role of a sister?

What do you want your children to know when it comes to each other?

What do you expect from them?

How do you expect them to conduct themselves in your absence in regard to each other?

NEVER LOVE ANYONE WHO TREATS YOU LIKE YOU'RE ORDINARY

— OSCAR WILDE

Boys, Birds & the Bees

How do you know when a boy/man loves you?

_____

_____

_____

_____

_____

_____

_____

_____

_____

_____

_____

_____

_____

_____

_____

_____

_____

_____

_____

_____

_____

_____

What does it mean to be in love?

What is the difference between being "In love" and being "In lust?"

How do you know when you are ready to have sex?

_____

_____

_____

_____

_____

_____

_____

_____

_____

_____

_____

_____

_____

_____

_____

_____

_____

_____

_____

_____

_____

What qualities will "The One" possess?

How can you tell that someone is "Mr. Wrong?"

What's the most important thing
to know about boys/men?

What do you wish you knew sooner about men?

How do you feel about "casual sex?"

What should you understand about contraception?

Is there ever a right time to not use condoms?

Is the number of sexual partners important?

How do you think your sexual behavior impacts how men view, and in turn, treat you?

What is your goal for dating?

What should you know about a man before getting serious?

What is the purpose of marriage?

What should you know about a man before getting married?

What should you know about a man before having children?

_____

_____

_____

_____

_____

_____

_____

_____

_____

_____

_____

_____

_____

_____

_____

_____

_____

_____

_____

_____

_____

_____

_____

WHATEVER IS GOOD FOR YOUR
SOUL—
DO THAT.

Divine Intervention

What does it mean to be spiritual?

Do you think that there is a difference between spirituality and religion?

Is one more important than the other?

What do you feel about God / "The Universe" / "High Power?"

Do you think it is important to communicate with God / "The Universe" / "High Power?"

How do you experience God / "The Universe" / "High Power?"

What do you always pray for?

What makes someone a "good person?"

START EACH DAY WITH A GRATEFUL HEART.

Attitude of Gratitude
What made you laugh or smile today?

How are you fortunate?

What are you grateful for?

What am I taking for granted that I am in fact grateful for?

What insights have I gained that I am grateful for?

What relationships am I grateful for?

What gifts do I offer to others am I grateful for?

A CHILD WITHOUT
EDUCATION,
IS LIKE A BIRD
WITHOUT WINGS.

— TIBETAN PROVERB

Education

What aspect of education is most important?

Does education need to be formal?

What is your dream job/career? Why?

Are you living that dream? Why or why not?

What helped / kept you from achieving that dream?

What is the most important aspect necessary for making sure your dreams come true?

What should you consider when making a decision about life goals?

If you had to choose would you choose beauty or brains?

How do you perceive failure?

MONEY DOESN'T IMPRESS
ME UNLESS IT'S

MY MONEY.

Money

What is the difference between a want and a need?

What are you trying to acquire with the money that you do have?

What do you feel the purpose of money is?

What do you want your children to know about money?

Do you value money? How?

What is your plan for passing down generational wealth?

What should every woman know about money?

Do money or gifts entitle a man to sex?

What are the advantages of making and having your own money?

What is a sure-fire way to get into debt?

How should you build credit? Why?

How do you think you could use your skills to gain wealth?

COMPARISON IS THE THIEF OF JOY.

— THEODORE ROOSEVELT

Stay In Your Lane

How do you stay focused on your goals?

How do you resist the temptation to compare yourself to others?

How do you define success?

What are your priorities?

Who or what do you live for?

What are the most important
things in your life? Why?

BE MORE CONCERNED WITH
YOUR CHARACTER THAN WITH
YOUR REPUTATION.

— JOHN WOODEN

Be a Woman of Character

What does your reputation mean to you?

How are character and reputation associated?

Does the current state of your reputation represent your character?

Do your circle of friends represent your core values?

Do you think it's important to protect your reputation?

How do you protect your reputation?

Do you think it is easier to preserve or to repair your reputation?

What are some character traits that you believe are important to possess?

DON'T FEEL ENTITLED TO ANYTHING YOU DIDN'T SWEAT AND STRUGGLE FOR

— MARIAN WRIGHT EDELMAN

No One Owes You Anything

Define entitlement.

How does one who believes he/she is entitled behave?

How does one come to the notion that they are entitled?

What are you entitled to?

www.ingramcontent.com/pod-product-compliance
Lightning Source LLC
Chambersburg PA
CBHW051837040426
42447CB00006B/578